DREAM
INTERPRETATIONS

An Hachette UK Company
www.hachette.co.uk

Material first published in *Understanding Dreams* in Great
Britain in 2005 by Hamlyn,
a division of Octopus Publishing Group Ltd
Carmelite House, 50 Victoria Embankment, London EC4Y 0DZ
www.octopusbooks.co.uk

This edition published in 2017 by Bounty Books, a division of
Octopus Publishing Group Ltd

ISBN 978-0-7537-3266-3

A CIP catalogue record for this book is available from the
British Library

Printed and bound in China

10 9 8 7 6 5 4 3 2 1

For the Bounty edition
Publisher: Lucy Pessell
Designer: Lisa Layton
Editor: Sarah Vaughan
Production Controller: Beata Kibil

DREAM
INTERPRETATIONS

*Helping you unlock the
meaning of your dreams*

DREAM INTERPRETATIONS

*Helping you unlock the
meaning of your dreams*

CONTENTS

INTRODUCTION

Most of us spend a third of our lives in the often surreal world of dreams, yet some still consider it to be as insignificant as a television soap era. Even if we awake from a nightmare that has seemed all too real, or a vivid dream teeming with what may be significant imagery, it is rare for us to reflect on it beyond breakfast, or make it more than the subject of an idle chat with friends.

And yet, our dreams are the sum of all that we have experienced and all that we have the potential to become. The dreams that we manage to recall are often couched in such obscure or surreal symbolism that we dismiss them as fantasies.

This might stem from the fact that most of us live our lives so fast that we do not have the time to savour the sensations. Our experiences and emotions are compressed into fleeting impressions that are reflected in our dreams in forms we are unable to appreciate.

Most of us suspect our dreams are reflections of our day-to-day activities and anxieties. And yet, we all have our share of puzzling dreams and disturbing nightmares which seem to suggest the potential for problem-solving and personal development. But which of your dreams are significant and how can you discover just what they are trying to tell you?

This book will help you explain your dreams, the common themes and their meanings.

THE FIVE STAGES OF SLEEP

Sleep can be divided into five distinct stages, the first four of which are classed as non-REM (rapid eye movement) sleep. These are characterized by thoughts rather than dreams.

• In the first, the 'alpha' stage, so called because the brain is producing alpha brainwaves, the heart rate slows and the muscles relax.

• The second stage is characterized by brief bursts of short-wave brain pulses. These invariably lead to the large, slow brainwaves of stage three.

• Stage three sees a further drop in the heartbeat and falls in blood pressure and body temperature.

• The fourth stage is known as 'delta' sleep – the lower frequency delta waves are produced in this relaxed state when the body is immobile.

• The fifth, and final, stage sees the drift into the REM phase where our most vivid dreams occur. This phase is also called paradoxical because the brainwaves indicate alertness, the adrenal glands secrete adrenaline in preparation for action, the muscles twitch and yet the body is limp and oblivious to external stimuli.

THE NEED TO DREAM

Scientists have found that for every 100 minutes of sleep, we experience 70–90 minutes of non-REM (rapid eye movement) sleep before drifting into the deeper REM dream state for 10–20 minutes.

The cycle repeats through the night, reflecting a similar cycle of day-dreaming at 90–100 minute intervals during waking hours. By waking and questioning volunteers about their dreams during both REM and non-REM sleep, scientists have found that detailed descriptions are elicited if a subject is awoken during REM sleep, while only sketchy impressions are gleaned if a volunteer is awoken during the non-REM phase.

Moreover, if a volunteer was repeatedly awoken during the REM phase, he or she would later compensate for the interruptions by indulging in longer periods of REM sleep when allowed to sleep on. In essence, this research suggests that we need to dream.

Sleep deprivation – All attempts to tamper with the sleep function in both animals and humans have had disturbing results. Animals kept awake for more than four days die from severe anaemia and hypothermia following behavioural disturbances ranging from restlessness and photophobia to eating disorders. Humans have a higher tolerance, but depriving people of sleep for more than two weeks leads to madness and finally death.

Dream deprivation – Researchers at the University of Chicago found that depriving someone of the dream phase of sleep had unpleasant results. Subjects were allowed to sleep but were woken when they entered the REM phase. As if to compensate, the REM phases increased in number as the experiment progressed to a point where the volunteers sank into REM sleep immediately they were allowed to sleep. When they were finally allowed a full night's sleep, they spent nearly 30 per cent of the night dreaming as opposed to the usual 10–20 per cent. Volunteers reported memory loss, lack of concentration, fatigue and irritability for a number of days.

ACTIVITY

EATING

The way the dreamer is eating should be seen as being equally important to what is being eaten.

Eating too much and in a hurry suggests a hunger for affection and a sense of insecurity. If you are on a diet, a dream 'binge' can be dismissed as wish-fulfilment. Eating meagrely and self-consciously indicates a lack of self-worth. Tearing savagely at the food symbolizes the desire to destroy something which is causing stress in waking life. A less frantic approach could mean the desire to ingest the strength of whatever is being eaten.

It is worthwhile examining the characteristics of the other participants, if there are any, as this hints at the need to integrate their qualities into the personality.

FALLING

The sensation of falling may be caused by biological changes during sleep, such as a sudden fall in blood pressure or an involuntary muscle twitch called a myoclonic spasm. Often, though, it indicates the detachment of the dream body from the physical.

If you experience only the imagery and not the sensation of falling the dream may indicate a fear of failure. This type of dream is particularly common among the career conscious and the financially insecure, although it can also occur in the dreams of those who fear for the security of their relationships.

FLYING

Flight is a common characteristic of lucid dreams in which we have a sudden realization that we are dreaming and that we are able to fly because it is 'only a dream'. These dreams are often exhilarating and accompanied by a sense of infinite possibilities and freedom which has led the mystically inclined to associate them with unconscious astral projection.

However, Freud theorized that flying dreams were the dreamer's recollections of being playfully tossed in the air during childhood or of swinging games, both of which awaken sexual feelings we subconsciously wish to recall.

If a difficult decision had been reached prior to falling asleep the flight symbol can be taken as an indication that the subconscious is saying that it is the right decision at the moment. If the dream follows a happy event or an achievement, it reflects a sense of confidence and also a deep sense of relief. To dream of being a passenger in an aircraft suggests that you are only prepared to explore new opportunities if you do not have to relinquish control or commit yourself too heavily. This dream has the opposite meaning if you are the pilot: that you feel in control of your life and are ready to 'spread your wings'.

CLIMBING

Climbing without reaching a goal indicates that we may be striving for something we suspect is unobtainable. These can be lofty ideals or unrealistic ambitions adopted in order to compensate for a childhood fear.

Alternatively, we may be seeking to rise above the mass of humanity for either altruistic or selfish ends. It would be worthwhile trying to re-enter the dream by active imagination, preferably upon waking, to understand the motive and to see what we are struggling towards or away from.

Climbing a ladder frequently represents professional or social ambitions, whereas a mountain represents life in general. Stairs had only a sexual connotation for Freud, but if the style, steepness and state of the stairs seems significant it can be seen as symbolic of the path ahead. Reaching the top suggests intellectual achievement, while descending the stairs indicates being ready to confront one's deepest fears.

Riding upwards in an elevator is suggestive of a rather functional attitude towards the sexual act. In any other environment, rising indicates increasing self-awareness. If the feeling is so real that it could almost be physical, then it is almost certainly an out-of-body-experience.

WALKING

Walking dreams are generally symbolic of life's journey and the progress made.

The most significant factor about them is the character of the landscape. If the scene is of pleasant countryside, this suggests peace of mind and acceptance that one is making the right decisions. If, however, it is an arduous trek through impenetrable jungle or through a busy city the dream might be indicating that your ambitions are unclear, or that you are trying to force your will against the natural flow of events.

Other factors to consider are whether you are continually looking back or striding forward with confidence. Moreover, is there a goal in sight? If so, what is it and how far away does it appear to be? Is the territory ahead difficult, treacherous and intimidating or clear and inviting?

BODY & SOUL

SPIRITUAL IMAGERY

The difficulty in interpreting the significance of religious images in dreams is that the unconscious may be drawing our attention to their esoteric (hidden or inner) rather than their exoteric (external or traditional) meaning. An understanding of both and their personal significance for the dreamer is therefore necessary to reveal the full extent of what the unconscious is trying to tell us.

Dreams that are strong in religious symbolism are more common to those who have denied their own spiritual nature in the belief that they are only rejecting religious dogma and conformism. As a result their inner being is trying to reassert itself by projecting the strongest images in its memory. Those who shun the material world and all its attractions will find themselves tormented in their dreams by gross caricatures of the instincts and passions they are attempting to suppress.

It is worth bearing in mind that the unconscious can also draw on religious imagery as a metaphor for secular concepts – the image of a biblical prophet, for example, to contrast past and present or use of an idol or divine figure to represent someone the dreamer subconsciously admires!

DEATH

Dreaming of the death of a loved one can serve as a release of the repressed hostility which occurs in even the most affectionate relationships. This mechanism originates from childhood when intense emotions could not be fully expressed and were not tempered with guilt or remorse. Dreaming of the death of a parent expresses the conflicting feelings common to all parent/child relationships, intensified by the mother/daughter rivalry for the father's affection and the father/son rivalry for attention from the mother.

Although the image of death can represent a wish on behalf of the dreamer to be rid of someone, it can also represent the dreamer's destructive tendencies – for example, his or her anger and frustration at life in general – and have nothing to do with the identity of the deceased. Some dreams of death do not symbolize the negative feelings of the dreamer for that person in waking life. The dreamer could be anticipating the absence of the loved one in order to examine the depth of their own feelings towards them.

If you dream of your own death a likely explanation is that you feel that the demands of life are draining you of your vitality or that you consider yourself to be unappreciated by others and may as well put yourself into a state where nothing more is demanded or expected of you. Death implies bereavement and a reassessment of life, suggesting a secret wish to have others feel guilty for not appreciating our qualities. If the atmosphere in the dream is positive, it may be that the dreamer's old attitudes are being peacefully put to rest in anticipation of a rebirth. More clues can be obtained from looking at the attitude of the mourners, if there are any, and the state of the body. If rigor mortis has set in the implication is a rigid attitude and crippling apprehension about what life might demand.

BLOOD

Blood is a universal symbol of the physical and spiritual life force.

For the Orthodox Christian it can refer to the blood of Christ and the act of taking communion with the divine aspect of the self. If in the dream there is a sense of repulsion at bathing, being baptized or covered in blood, however, the suggestion is a fear of taking responsibility and entering into adulthood.

For a man to dream that he is bleeding from a wound the suggestion is fear of emasculation, humiliation and loss of virility. The same dream for a woman suggests the fear of losing her virginity or the memory of that event. Wounds can also represent emotional trauma, especially fear of being emotionally 'drained' by a lover, or of suffering self-inflicted wounds through rash actions.

If the wounds leave a scar, the implication is that the emotional effects have not yet been dealt with. If they are seen to heal, this is reassurance that the dreamer has the capacity for self-healing.

LIMBS

Limbs can have a phallic connotation. The loss of a limb may represent loss of virility for a male or loss of virginity for a female. Being dismembered symbolizes the fear that one's life is coming apart, although it may simply indicate the necessity for reassessment.

Outstretched arms imply a need for help, support or acceptance. In a dream of this kind it would be necessary to consider whose arms are reaching out to whom and for what purpose.

Legs are more likely to appear as pictorial puns on well-known phrases. For example, if the dreamer has been drinking heavily they may dream that they are literally 'legless'.

Similarly, dreaming that your feet are frozen is likely to play on the phrase 'having cold feet', implying second thoughts concerning an agreement.

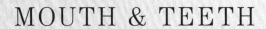

MOUTH & TEETH

The mouth is a potent symbol of our demands and our needs, although Freudians would limit these to sexual desires, seeing the mouth itself as a symbol of the female genitalia and the tongue as a symbol of the penis.

If the focus of the dream is on eating, attention should be paid to the significance of what is being eaten and the way it is being consumed.

A full set of healthy teeth is a symbol of our ability to eat whatever we choose and thus sustain ourselves. Losing teeth in a dream usually represents a fear of becoming helpless. Such imagery can be particularly distressing because it implies there might be something rotten or diseased in a sensitive area of our lives or body. However, if this image is accompanied by a feeling of relief, the inference to be drawn from the dream is that the problem festering away in the psyche has finally been removed.

Teeth falling out easily in the dream is a flashback to childhood when the loss of teeth was a sign of impending maturity and the end of a comparatively carefree existence. Perhaps the dreamer has a secret wish to return to those carefree days? The loss of teeth accompanied by embarrassment and anxiety indicates that we subconsciously fear what old age might bring – helplessness, impoverishment, undesirability, ill-health and dependency. However, as our teeth help shape our features, yet another interpretation can be read into this image – fear of 'losing face'.

Freudians would also see a sexual connotation, with the teeth representative of aggressive sexuality, especially in dreams where the act of biting is a feature. Conversely, a dream in which a woman swallows a tooth would be seen by Freudians as being symbolic of her desire for or fear of pregnancy.

COLOURS &
NUMBERS

BLACK & WHITE

Pure white light is said to be a true reflection of divine primordial energy. White is associated with energy and is used in Indian esoteric philosophies to represent the highest chakra in the etheric body. To dream of white is to dream of the highest potential of whatever the dreamer is imagining. In psychological terms white symbolizes the importance of the intellect.

Light is reduced by degrees until the polar opposite of white is reached – black, in essence the absence of light, associated with negativity, evil and death. Black is associated with death in Western society because it signifies that the divine light of the life force has departed. Crows, ravens, cats and even black stallions are traditionally considered to be creatures of ill omen. For orthodox Christians blackbirds are the symbol of temptation. Christian and Muslim clerics wear black to symbolize that they have renounced the attractions of the world. In esoteric and occult circles black is held to be the colour of the physical world, being the densest colour and our world being the densest plane of energy. Black has a secondary symbolic significance and that is secrecy. The unconscious might shield a person in the dream in deep shadow or cover an object with a black cloth to indicate that the dreamer is hiding a secret, or that the other person or object is concealing a secret.

Because most of our dreams are in colour, it can be assumed that black and white will be used to highlight duality and contrast. Figures dressed predominantly in black or white stand out against a crowd more effectively than any other colour combination and so will be used by the unconscious to draw the dreamer's attention to individuals clothed in either of these colours.

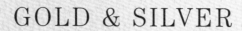

GOLD & SILVER

Gold has many associations with wealth, refinement and divinity. In the ancient world it was considered the purest and most precious of minerals because of its association with the sun, its radiant beauty and for the fact that it could not be corrupted by rust. Gold symbolized the vibrant male sun god and thus strength. Through the ages it embodied all the attributes of heavenly glory and earthly power. It was the chosen metal in the making of sacred objects and its creation from base material was the ultimate goal of the alchemists.

To dream of a person adorned in gold is to be thinking of them in the highest terms. Such a dream signifies secret respect and admiration for that person rather than affection. To dream of mining for gold indicates that something of great significance has been buried in the unconscious. The discovery of more gold than we can carry in a dream suggests that we are trying to do more than is practical in the mistaken belief that activity equals achievement.

In the ancient world, silver was regarded as the second most precious metal. It was the complement of gold, representing the cool mysterious feminine goddess personified as the moon. To dream of silver is considered to indicate purity, chastity and the talent to charm (hence the popular term 'to be silver-tongued').

BLUE & VIOLET

There is a strong folk tradition in Europe which associates the colour blue with fidelity. This is echoed by the Chinese belief that the appearance of the colour in a dream is a portent of a happy and enduring marriage. To dream of a vivid blue object, cloudless sky or serene seascape can be interpreted as a message from the unconscious that the veil to the subconscious can now be lifted at will. From a psychological perspective light blue is most commonly associated with the sky and the sea, both of which are elements concerned with mutable emotions. The association of the colour blue with the sky is also suggestive of elevated, spiritual thoughts and intuition, implying that the unconscious is likely to be urging the dreamer to trust his or her intuition in a matter where the emotions are concerned. A dream featuring the colour of calm seas and fair skies appears to promise a positive outcome.

Despite its popular association with melancholy, deep blue is a calming and healing colour associated with the throat chakra in Eastern philosophies. Its presence in a dream implies the need for self-expression for the purpose of healing oneself and others who might be touched by the beauty of whatever is created. Perhaps the dreamer has crippling doubts about his or her ability or self-worth and could be healed through some form of creative expression.

Violet is a transitional colour in practical, psychological and spiritual terms, being a blend of red (symbolizing physical energy, fire and action) with blue (symbolizing the sea or sky, the celestial and the intellect). In ancient Rome violets were worn on the heads of banqueting guests in order to cool and calm them. This custom led to the colour becoming associated with the desirable qualities of moderation and a balance of passion with aspiration.

GREEN & BROWN

Green has a number of negative associations such as envy, inexperience and jealousy, but it is also the universal symbol of spring, freshness and vitality.
In occult philosophy it is seen as the colour of harmony, balance and regeneration as embodied in nature. It corresponds to the quality of energy at the heart chakra and is the frequency between the physical and the spiritual realms. This is one reason why we seek to find harmony, balance and peace in a garden and in the countryside.

In practical terms it is the colour we have come to associate with safety and permission to proceed, as in the green of traffic lights and the international green cross adopted by the pharmaceutical industry. Green has dual meanings in dreams – lushness and coolness – and requires careful interpretation. A dream featuring a significant green element might be urging you to get on with a pet project or seek fresh opportunities further afield. Or, it might be cautioning against the belief that the grass is always greener on the other side of the fence!

Brown is associated with the earth and with many hibernating animals. It may appear in dreams to symbolize a period of inactivity and rest prior to sowing the seeds of the next harvest in life.

If we dream of someone in mousy brown clothes this could indicate that we consider them to be shy, modest and unassuming, although appearances can be deceptive!
The usual meaning is impoverishment, because brown is the colour of barren soil and the habits of poor Christian monks.

RED, ORANGE & YELLOW

Red corresponds to the lower chakra at the base of the spine and is the colour of physical energy, of action and the passions. In the physical world it is the colour we associate with blood, fire, heat and danger and yet the more pastel shades are considered symbolic of the finer aspects of physical energy (as in those energies needed in sport) while the darker reds symbolize the more intense emotions such as passion and anger. It is no arbitrary association or coincidence that has led to the heart, as the seat of the passions, being popularly but erroneously depicted as red.

Orange comes between the red of the physical dimension and the yellow of the mental aspects of our being and is the colour of positive emotions. Orange is associated with fire and the setting sun, both suggesting controlled passion. Orange blossoms were once bound in bridal bouquets as tokens of fertility, and the Chinese traditionally eat oranges at New Year as symbols of good fortune.

Yellow is the second of the primary colours. In ancient times it was associated with the life-giving force and healing rays of the sun. It corresponds to the third chakra at the level of the solar plexus which is associated with the emotions. In dreamlore yellow is more likely to reflect nervous energy, repressed emotions, intellectual achievement and ambition. If your dream features someone in yellow, this person could represent someone who excites strong emotions within you, perhaps because you strongly disagree with their opinions or consider them to be overly critical and lacking in spontaneity.

ODD & EVEN NUMBERS

Odd numbers are generally representative of the mysterious, intuitive, unknown and unpredictable elements in life, whereas even numbers represent the familiar and practical everyday elements.

However, in ancient Greece even numbers were considered to symbolize feminine, passive qualities, and odd numbers the active and masculine qualities.

DATES

Dreaming of a particular date on a calendar, in a desk diary or newspaper may be a reminder of an important forthcoming event such as a birthday, job interview or anniversary. Such a dream could also be precognitive.

It is not uncommon for a housebuyer to dream of the number of the house he or she will later own. In drawing the dreamer's attention to a future day, week or month the dream might be forewarning of changes ahead.

ZERO, ONE & TWO

Drawn as a circle, zero represents infinity. In ancient Babylonia, India and Arabia zero was seen as a sacred symbol of the creator, the essence of all things. Its appearance as a significant element in a dream would indicate that all potential is contained within but that the dreamer is waiting for ideal conditions. Its reverse meaning, as a symbol of nothingness, is a warning not to wait too long before taking action.

The number one has traditionally symbolized unity and perfection as envisaged in the form of an omnipotent deity. A phallic shape, it can also represent active masculinity and force. One can also suggest the first stage of a journey. More commonly it implies aloofness or isolation. In a competitive context, it promises success and the confidence to put oneself first.

Two signifies duality and balance. The symbolism and context will clarify whether the twin aspects, often the dreamer and his or her partner, are in opposition or harmony. If the number is expressed in the form of objects the implication is one of contrast, such as the benefits of reflection as opposed to action. The dreamer should note how the objects appear in relation to each other. If they are seen side by side the configuration suggests equality, whereas if one is behind the other then it implies that one aspect of the dreamer or one person in the relationship is in the shadow of the other.

The number two can also appear as a significant symbol in dreams when the dreamer has a choice to make between two equally appealing alternatives.

TEN & ONE HUNDRED

As an image the number 10 is suggestive of contrast, with the straight vertical line appearing in opposition to the circle, and is traditionally seen as symbolizing male (1) and female (0). At a deeper level it may be hinting at finality, with the line seen as a barrier impeding the circle's progress and the circle as an image of wholeness and harmony. Perhaps you have completed a phase of your life and can now go no further on your present course?

In the esoteric tradition, ten corresponds to the ten spheres on the Tree of Life, a symbol of the various qualities or attributes of the divine which are reflected in the human psyche and physical body. Dreaming of the number ten is therefore of great spiritual significance for those actively seeking enlightenment. A dream in which this meaningful number features would suggest that the various elements in the dreamer's life are in balance and that a new level of understanding is about to be reached.

Pictorially 100 suggests an emotional triad, with two women vying for the attention of one male. A more common interpretation is that the number simply stands for an uncountable number, for 'many'.

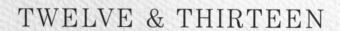

TWELVE & THIRTEEN

Twelve signifies celestial order and completion of a cycle of activity in terms of time. It may be symbolized by the twelve signs of the zodiac, a calendar representing the twelve months of the year or a clock representing the twelve hours of the day. In some cultures, twelve is the age of maturity and responsibility when a child is accepted by the community as an adult. The sense of self-development and new-found status this represents may express itself in dream symbolism, such as receiving the gift of a watch with the hands fixed at twelve o'clock or, as is often the case, with no hands at all!

Thirteen has become a number of ill omen due to its many negative associations: Judas Iscariot was counted as the thirteenth man present at the Last Supper; the devil has been imagined to be the thirteenth guest of a witches' coven; in pagan mythology the Scandinavian god of light, Balder, was slain at a banquet in Valhalla by an unexpected thirteenth guest, the intruder Loki; in ancient times the addition of an extra, thirteenth, 'month' to complete the early lunar calendars was considered unlucky.

The superstition attached to the number thirteen has been further enforced by other 'meaningful coincidences', such as the fact that the thirteenth Tarot card in the major arcana is Death. However, a more accurate interpretation of this card and of the number thirteen appearing in a dream is that both signify change. To dream that you are entering a house or room numbered thirteen or ascending to the thirteenth floor, indicates anxiety concerning coming changes, but also an overwhelming curiosity to explore new possibilities.

PERSONALITIES

MOTHER & FATHER

Dreaming of a mother figure is to face the maternal instinct, namely the desire to nurture and protect the young. It could mean that the unconscious is encouraging us to comfort and nurture the 'inner child'. This is especially the case if we have been too hard on ourselves or have temporarily lost the child-like love of life. However, there are always two sides to each figure and the unconscious may use a mother figure to admonish the dreamer for an act the dreamer knew was wrong.

The unconscious does not respect political correctness and it could project an image of the mother dutifully carrying out domestic chores to remind a male dreamer of his obligations and responsibilities as a father or son.

On a deeper level the mother is an aspect of female energy, which can assume a form known as the Terrible Mother, often appearing as a wicked queen, witch or a black widow spider. In these forms the mother embodies the negative characteristics of the over-protective and possessive matriarch who smothers her children's potential for growth. A woman who lives her life through her children, sacrificing her happiness in the belief that they would not survive in the world without her, may also dream of herself in this form. If so, it is a warning to her not to neglect her own needs.

In his positive aspect the father represents respect for authority, protection, acceptable standards of behaviour and guidance. His dark side is the ogre, a strict disciplinarian who seeks to repress individuality and constrain the dreamer's uniqueness with rigid, irrational rules.

SHADOW & PURSUER

The Shadow is that part of ourselves which we choose to ignore and which reacts by haunting our dreams. For example, an introvert will often dream of acting in an outrageous fashion, while an extrovert may compensate for time spent impressing others by taking time for him or herself. If we are able to recognize the Shadow when it appears and gradually integrate rather than deny its existence, it will cease to haunt our dreams.

Any character who threatens us in a dream is likely to symbolize our Shadow. Although the appearance of the pursuer or intruder may be disturbing, it is important to realize that it symbolizes an aspect of the personality which has been denied and is literally haunting the dreamer in the hope of being recognized and integrated into the personality.

The best way to achieve this is to programme the mind each night before going to sleep by repeating to yourself that when the pursuer appears you will stop, face it and ask it what it wants of you. This move almost always guarantees a revealing answer and puts a stop to the nightmares.

AUTHORITY OR MILITARY FIGURE

Authority figures are often substitutes for the dreamer's father although they can also symbolize the anonymous forces of the state. Teachers can appear to remind us how vulnerable we once felt and can still feel when challenged about something which we have not considered carefully enough. Judges and policemen can stand in for our own conscience concerning an act which we knew to be wrong when we committed it.

Respite dream will not be achieved until we acknowledge this wrong. If the dreamer thinks he has been unjustly criticized by a parent or teacher, then an authority figure can appear as someone who is not to be trusted.

Any individual or group of figures representing the armed forces is symbolic of our attempt to constrain our aggressive impulses. The more active the characters are, the fiercer is the struggle between the aggressive impulse and the fear of losing control of emotions. A dream centring on the importance of rank or battle formations, indicates anxiety regarding orderliness in waking life and a desire that life should conform to our concept of right and wrong.

CROWD OR MOB

A crowd usually appears in dreams as an irrational force opposed to the will and beliefs of the dreamer. It can represent the world at large, the community in which the dreamer lives and works or his or her own subconscious. If you are jeered at by the mob in your dream, it indicates that your ideas on a particular subject have not been properly thought through. If you feel threatened by the anonymity of the crowd, this implies that you feel pressured to conform or fear criticism about your views or image in waking life.

To become part of the crowd can indicate a desire to be accepted, even at the cost of losing your own identity. More commonly, this dream can signify a need to escape responsibilities. In one of the more disturbing dreams of this type, the dreamer is caught up and carried along by a surging crowd. This symbolizes a fear of losing control and being swept along by the momentum of events.

PRIESTESS OR WISE
OLD MAN

The priestess personifies the quality of intuition. Her appearance in dreams indicates an awakening of the subtler, psychic senses or the need to attend to the needs of the inner self, which may be overwhelmed by materialistic concerns.

Her dark side is the witch. As a dream symbol, she signifies a person wrapped up in their own fantasies and suspicious of the motives of others. Her appearance can suggest a fear of persecution, but as with the true witches of the past she may hold secrets, which could be beneficial to the dreamer.

Male potential is embodied in the figure known as The Wise Old Man. He is likely to make his first appearance in a man's dreams from the age of 40, when most men begin to seriously consider the meaning of their lives and look to their own potential rather than to their father for inspiration and insight. The appearance of this figure in a dream is extremely significant, and any advice given in the dream should be considered very seriously indeed.

SIGNIFICANT
OBJECTS &
SIGNIFICANT
SITUATIONS

SEXUAL SYMBOLS

Any long, pointed object which can penetrate another or is capable of emitting liquid under pressure could be a phallic symbol. For that reason certain tools, weapons, gardening equipment and farming implements could be used by the unconscious as obscure symbols of the male genitalia. Even such innocuous objects as umbrellas, bottles, certain musical instruments, water pistols, hoses and syringes could have sexual connotations in the dreamscape.

Milk and other liquids may appear as symbols of semen, although dreaming of watching helplessly as a precious fluid drains away through a crack in the ground could simply be expressing a fear of losing one's vitality or of regretting past mistakes (hence the saying 'crying over spilt milk'). Playing with a ball could reflect curiosity regarding male masturbation, although for men it could also have an entirely 'innocent' meaning in recalling the leisure and simple pleasures of childhood. Hollow objects and containers often symbolize the vagina or the womb.

BOOKS

In waking life we associate books with knowledge, but in the dreamworld they symbolize our memories. Books bound in leather and elaborately embossed symbolize treasured memories, but could also imply a certain nostalgia and sentimentality which might be misplaced. Well-thumbed paperbacks, which are yellowing, curling at the edges and cracked at the spine are symbolic of a hard life in which there has been little time for dwelling on the past. In this case memories are merely data banks of useful facts and experience and the dream is signifying that the answer to whatever troubles us at present or in the future is to be found in our past.

KEYS

Keys are symbols of the solution to a problem, the nature of which should be obvious from the context and details of the dream.

What is needed is to follow the dream through to see what the key will open. If this does not happen in the dream itself, simply re-enter the dream as soon as possible upon waking and allow the events to unfold effortlessly as if it was a daydream. If the key fits a door, it suggests the solution lies in a change of circumstance, although the nature of the room you enter could give further clues. If it fits the lock of a box or chest the solution could lie in something which has been suppressed or simply forgotten.

Again, the symbolic significance of the furniture should give further clues. If the key fits a piano, Freudian analysts would probably insist that the dream has sexual significance and that the dreamer wishes to 'perform' with someone they want to make 'beautiful music with' or who they seek to dominate. Alternatively, it could be that he or she simply wants to develop a talent which has been neglected for some time. However, it might also be that the problem being pondered has no simple answer and so the piano keys will symbolize the innumerable variations and possibilities with which the dreamer can play around in search of harmony in his or her life. If the dream does not resolve itself satisfactorily, it might be important to recall where the key was found. If, for example, it was found under a bed, it could signify that the dreamer needs rest and relaxation. If it was discovered in a garden under a bush, it could signify that the dreamer needs a period of reflection in a quiet and inspiring spot.

MACHINES

Heavy machines with moving parts invariably represent the body, specifically the stomach. Complex electronic devices such as computers frequently symbolize the human brain. It may be that warnings of impending physical problems first appear in dreams as images of overloaded or rusting machinery before the first symptoms are felt. Stress or intense mental fatigue could be reflected in dreams centring on fused or temperamental electrical devices. If the dream reflects anxiety over a particular problem, it could be useful to re-enter it and ask the computer which solution it recommends, or what the consequences of taking various forms of action would be.

If you find yourself operating machinery which is carrying out monotonous tasks, a possible interpretation might be that life has become routine and predictable. In such cases the unconscious is warning that you are living life 'mechanically', motivated by habit rather than curiosity, ambition or emotion.

MONEY OR TREASURE

Most of us believe that if we have enough money it will protect us from everything that we see as being negative in life, even though we know this is untrue. In our dreams we equate health, social status and even our sexual potency with the amount of money we possess or desire. Not having enough money symbolizes a fear of losing face, influence or power, while winning large amounts of cash symbolizes a need for respect and security and perhaps also an unconscious desire to be recognized and acknowledged as being superior to our neighbours or colleagues.

If we have recently endured emotional upsets or ill-health we may dream of receiving an unexpected windfall to make everything right again and to cushion us from the effects of any future shocks. To dream of bargaining, arguing about money or profiting from financial deals is often a reflection of a need to outwit someone we know in waking life who we believe is more fortunate or more talented than we are. Such dreams indicate an inferiority complex and immaturity which is expressed in the need to flaunt wealth as if it was proof of personal value.

Dreaming of being forced to give away or spend large amounts of money to settle debts implies a guilt complex and the need 'to pay' for what we have done to restore the balance. Hoarding money has the same implications as it does in real life – a distrust of others, a fear of the future and of having to rely on our own resources. To dream of going on a spending spree is expressing a desire to shake off inhibitions and indulge the senses and live life to the full, regardless of whether or not our affections are returned.

BEING CAUGHT OR TRAPPED

Dreaming of being entangled or ensnared in ropes and cables, is symbolic of the dreamer's fear of being restricted from doing whatever he or she wants to do. It can also express a real fear of being overwhelmed by unexpected commitments, most commonly financial or family-related ones because these are the ones from which we have the most trouble freeing ourselves.

Dreaming of being trapped by falling rubble or trees suggests that emotional or other pressures are threatening to 'get on top' of you and pin you down. The best way to exorcise such anxieties is to face the facts during daylight and accept the consequences of whichever option you decide upon.

Being locked in a room is a more complex case because it is necessary to discover what led you to the location and who locked you in. Being imprisoned can be symbolic of a sense of being cut off from the outside world, from society, the family or peer group. Discovering who imprisoned you can, therefore, give a valuable clue to the cause of the dream. In recalling the events or in re-entering the dream on waking to resolve it, you may discover that you entrapped yourself, through a craving for something which you secretly desire but you know is not good for you.

NAKEDNESS

If being undressed in your dream is a pleasurable sensation it suggests that you regard social conventions as artificial and are making a show of shedding your inhibitions. You may also consider the other people in the scene to be hypocritical in their conventional attitudes and want to shock them. If, however, you are embarrassed by being naked, in your dream, whether you are alone or before others, then you are likely to be manifesting a fear of being seen to be inadequate or looking foolish.

The question is whether we believe it is our 'real self' which is being exposed as inadequate, or the persona, the façade that we hide behind. If the latter, then perhaps the unconscious is encouraging us to drop our pretence and expose our true nature to the world in confidence. This is likely if we have been overly defensive or secretive and are beginning to realize that this is causing us more problems than it solves. Such dreams may also occur if we are harbouring any guilt and are unconsciously seeking to unburden ourselves and 'come clean'.

The reactions of others can be equally significant. For example, if we find ourselves naked in a public place and no one appears to notice us, it could signify that we are too self-conscious and the dream is a compensatory reaction. But if the onlookers point and jeer, it betrays a fear of being rejected after trusting others with our true feelings.

In rare cases the image of seeing oneself naked may even be symbolic of the sensation of freedom which we feel on leaving the physical body, albeit briefly and unconsciously, during sleep as consciousness views the body as a second skin or overcoat.

EXAMS, INTERVIEWS & AUDITIONS

Taking an exam is one of the most common anxiety dreams and one which has been frequently dismissed as being merely a fear of returning to the constraints and pressures of school days. The more likely explanation for such dreams is that we are having doubts about our current career or a relationship and so our unconscious is revisiting a time when we faced equal anxiety as a means of reassurance. The purpose of this may be to remind the conscious mind that we overcame our fear to pass this earlier test, or, if we failed the exam, then at least such traumas are long gone just as this current problem will be in time.

To dream of sitting an exam that one is unprepared for is indicative of an unconscious anxiety concerning the overall course of one's life. It is as if the unconscious is rehearsing for the final judgement, regardless of whether or not the dreamer has a conscious belief in the hereafter.

Although dreams of being tongue-tied during an audition or late for an important interview are more common among people who are constantly being tested in a competitive profession, they can also haunt us at times when we feel that we are losing control of life. Through such dreams the unconscious is warning of what might happen if we continue to drive ourselves too hard or take on too many commitments.

Dreams of this kind can be the result of our irrational need to explain past failures as being entirely our fault and may be stimulated by the memory of minor mistakes for which we are still punishing ourselves.

PURSUIT

It cannot be assumed that whatever is pursuing us in our dreams is intent on harming us or that we are the helpless victims of monsters from the unconscious. It may well be that we are running from responsibilities which we once took on quite willingly, but which we now realize are preventing us from pursuing our own self-interest. Even if we recognize our pursuer, it may only be standing in as the acceptable face of whatever is really troubling us. The real culprit is more than likely to be the everyday pressures and problems that we have unconsciously agreed to take on in order to evolve as personalities.

If we are pursuing something or somebody it could be that we still have an unresolved desire for, or attachment to, something which we cannot accept is beyond our comprehension or attainment. If we re-enter the dream on waking we may finally catch up with this elusive person or object and discover that it is something we no longer need and have only been pursuing out of a long-established habit. It is not unknown for the dreamer to find that what is being evaded is an aspect of him- or herself, the Shadow, or something which is desired but if obtained may be impossible to cope with.

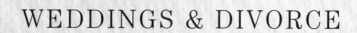

WEDDINGS & DIVORCE

Wedding dreams are less likely to be precognitive than merely wish fulfilment fantasies or symbols of a commitment to something of significance in our lives. This something is not necessarily a relationship. The image is being used by the unconscious to reinforce the seriousness of the situation and our responsibility to the enterprise. If the wedding makes the dreamer anxious, it could be reflecting an anxiety about making a commitment. In rare cases wedding dreams can symbolize the integration of two complementary aspects of the dreamer's own personality such as his or her practical and creative qualities.

As with dreams of marriage the theme of divorce can be stimulated by a desire to break free from an attachment or commitment which is not necessarily connected with a personal relationship. We may be frustrated with a situation in waking life and putting all our energy into something which the unconscious is suggesting might be better left alone.

Such dreams may even occur to single people who are considering making a commitment to something or somebody. In effect, the individual is acting out in the safety of the imagination how he or she would cope with failure.

TRANSPORT & TRAVEL

ROADS

In general, natural paths and tracks represent the landscape of an inner journey, whereas man-made streets symbolize the road ahead in waking life. Winding lanes can indicate a need for relaxation, to 'stretch one's legs' to escape an intense situation. Alternatively, the scene might reflect deep satisfaction to have reached the psychological equivalent of open country after a period when one has been restricted and under stress.

Town and city streets generally appear in dreams when the dreamer's life is complicated and the way ahead is not clear. The maze of criss-crossing, interconnecting streets and jungle of signs and lights symbolizes inner conflict and confusion. Dreams of driving in the city are often indicative of indecision and being faced with an overwhelming number of choices. City and town driving is a series of starts and stops, of giving way and being alert to the impulsive actions of others. That is why the setting is useful to the unconscious for preparing us for the unpredictable.

Cul-de-sacs symbolize the end of a phase in one's life, a dead end. A fork in the road can indicate a parting of the ways from someone who has come a long way on the journey of life with you. A fast-flowing motorway indicates a life of broad horizons and a choice of fulfilling opportunities. The image also suggests that it will be a long journey before the ultimate goal is reached and that this is not necessarily known to the dreamer.

If the dream journey is set on a busy motorway and we are hemmed in on all sides the implication is that we are under stress in waking life and being forced to follow the dictates of others, to run with the pack rather than risk asserting our individuality.

AEROPLANES, GLIDERS
& BALLOONS

Dreams of flying by balloon and glider can reflect a longing to be free of terrestrial troubles and instead experience the tranquillity of the celestial realm. More negatively the sense may be taken to mean 'take flight' and flee from obligations. They can also symbolize our lofty ambitions, a desire to soar above the multitude and the mundane or a desire to have a new perspective on a world which we find confusing and intimidating.

The distinguishing feature of flight over other forms of transport is that it involves leaving 'Mother Earth'. Dreams of flying or of waiting impatiently for a flight could be a wish to break free of a dominating female figure.

But unless we have a fear of flying, in which case the dream is attempting to help us face the absurdity of our phobia, aircraft imagery is more likely to be reflecting the sensation of being out of the body during the sleep state and not simply a stage in a symbolic journey.

SHIPS, BOATS & RAFTS

As water is the element symbolic of the emotions and often divides one land mass from another, so dreams featuring ships, rafts and boats invariably symbolize difficult emotional transitions from one significant stage in life to another. The boat represents the physical body within whose protective shell we weather the storms of experience. A small rowing boat or raft would signify that the dreamer feels exposed to the buffeting winds of fate. A fishing boat, cargo vessel or tanker would indicate that life is considered to be all work, offering little opportunity for leisure. A cruise liner would indicate a relaxed attitude to life in general, and possibly a sensual nature. A ferry, with its car decks and association with making short journeys, would suggest that the dreamer is reluctant to let go of worldly 'baggage', possessions, attitudes, beliefs and values at a time when these need to be jettisoned for him to make a critical change.

To find the boat in disrepair indicates that we might not be ready to take the trip, no matter how much we might long to reach the far shore. If you discover fellow passengers or a crew aboard who appear willing to join you in the adventure, this implies that all aspects of your personality are prepared for a change that will benefit the whole person. If you discover that the passengers view you with suspicion or the crew are drunk or mutinous, the inference is that there is resistance to change and maturity from the Shadow and less developed aspects of the self.

If the crossing is difficult and the obstacles formidable it indicates that there is inner resistance to change and that a great resolve is needed to overcome this. The meaning of common expressions such as 'it's all plain sailing', 'sailing close to the wind' and 'having plans scuppered' will give further clues as to the significance of the images in waking life.

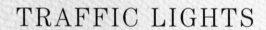

TRAFFIC LIGHTS

Being stuck at traffic lights may simply be a warning against being impatient, by forcing us to re-live our frustration and seeing how absurd it looks in the dreamworld, a surreal world where there is no time or purpose. It could also be drawing our attention to the fact that we might be relying on others too much before we act. If we are stuck with the lights at red for a long time, it might be telling us to slow down and take things easier. If the lights stay on yellow, it is probably indicating that we need to spend more time in preparation before presenting our ideas for approval. A green light is encouraging us to go ahead without waiting for a signal from other people who may mean well but whose values and concept of life will be different from our own.

Breaking down, or not being able to start the engine, at a junction while the lights are constantly changing, suggests indecision, specifically an inability to proceed with anything without first getting other people's opinions and then, having done so, not being able to act on them for fear of making the wrong decision.

CARS

In general the act of driving a car represents the urge to make our own way in the world using our own resources and often with an element of impatience. Certain schools of analysis would see a car as a symbol of a woman that the dreamer wishes to possess sexually. This is reflected in the fact that most men speak of their car in feminine terms, but in most dreams cars serve as a wish for greater social status and respect. They can also be seen as vehicles of our own dream ego, as an extension of our driving passions, physique, preoccupations and emotions.

A study of the car's condition tells us a lot about our attitudes to these. For example, any concerns about the body work, reflected in rust or dulling paint work and chrome, could be an indication of concerns about ageing and getting out of condition.

Dreams of tinkering with the engine would be reflecting unconscious concerns about the heart, while problems with the electronics would be warning against stress and overwork. A sleek, flashy car crammed with parking tickets, cigarette butts, empty cans and CDs suggests someone who is eager to appear successful, fashionable and fun, but who is really disorganized and overly keen to impress because they lack confidence.

Being driven by someone else can have a multitude of meanings. We might wish to cruise through life with others making the decisions, in which case the car is likely to be a luxury model or limousine, or we may like to be surprised by life and not wish to know where we are going. Alternatively, we may fear that someone else will take control of our life and lead us into unknown territory. Perhaps that other person, symbolized by the driver, is our own Shadow? Or it may be that our own impulses are driving us and that we feel unable to take control and steer ourselves back on the 'straight and narrow'.

THE WORLDS WITHIN & WITHOUT

PLACES OF WORSHIP

Churches, temples, mosques and other places of worship are often interpreted as religious symbols. However, they are more likely to represent actual places of introspection and reflection within the individual, an inner sanctuary within the psyche free from associations with any specific tradition or belief. As such, these images can indicate a real experience, the moment when the veil between the conscious and the unconscious mind is temporarily drawn aside and we make a connection with our Higher Self.

If the dreamer is not bound by religious conditioning the scene in the dream might instead be a beautiful garden, a deserted beach or any place of natural beauty and serenity. Such a dream does not necessarily have spiritual significance. The quality of the experience will indicate whether you have had a 'regular' dream or achieved a higher state of consciousness. With the latter there will be a sensation of having entered a 'sacred space' and a strong 'afterglow' will persist after waking.

Such 'dreams' can convey a specific message verbally or through a symbolic image. Often, however, their purpose is simply to reassure us that we are not alone in waking life.

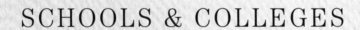

SCHOOLS & COLLEGES

Our attitudes towards society and the state are largely the result of our experience of school, which, as a closed community with its own rules and values, can be seen as offering a rehearsal for later life. The intensity and sensitivity of childhood and adolescent emotions is often used by the unconscious to focus us on the causes and consequences of conflict in adulthood. However, when interpreting dreams with a school setting, it should be remembered that the school's values may have coloured our own. Such dreams may be trying to resolve a conflict between the standards of achievement demanded by the school and our expectations of ourselves.

To dream of being back at school long after you have left is a very common theme. You may be uncertain of which way to proceed at present and have returned to schooldays to reassess the future from that perspective. Or, you may be afraid that someone in authority (symbolized by the school), possibly a parent, may wipe out the progress you have made in adult life and return you to a position of dependence.

If the dream is set in a college or university, the implication is that there were lessons to be learnt from past experiences which are relevant to the present situation and that they should be considered carefully before you commit yourself to a particular course of action.

BANKS & LIBRARIES

Banks often enter our dreams transformed from custodians of our money to symbols of authority whom we feel we must appease. No matter how much money we have in reality the banks in our dreams will assume a form that is certain to undermine our emotional stability, security and self-assurance. Whenever we become too complacent, particularly with regard to having our emotions under control, the unconscious will use our ambiguous attitude to officialdom in general and such institutions in particular to force us to face the unpalatable fact that we can be easily destabilized if faced with irrational demands, unreasonable expectations or false accusations. It is common for a financially secure person to dream that his bank manager has called him in to demand the repayment of a loan or overdraft that he does not have in waking life, or to dream that his property and possessions are being repossessed without any reason being given.

In the real world we associate libraries primarily with knowledge. In the dreamworld of the unconscious they symbolize memories. To search for a book is to search for a specific memory or detail. To stagger under a pile of heavy books or see yourself furiously leafing through books while the staff are waiting to close for the night signifies being burdened with a memory that has been repressed. If you are repeatedly plagued by such dreams and awake from them anxious and troubled, try re-entering the dream and calmly imagine yourself asking the librarian to help you search. The library staff may be mere authority figures, but if the dream is an intensely emotional one, they are more likely to be aspects of your personality, probably the part that holds the repressed memory. If this is the case, they can be encouraged to give up their secret. If you suspect the memory is painful or traumatic, you should seek professional help to uncover it.

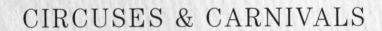

CIRCUSES & CARNIVALS

Such settings could be encouraging the dreamer to be less intense and return to the carefree attitude of childhood; toys in a dream may be conveying a similar message. However, there is also a certain melancholic quality associated with such places, where the clowns might be seen to bear fixed smiles, where wild animals perform tricks for our amusement and the rootless lifestyle of stall holders and performers symbolizes the outsider.

One of the most common dreams with a circus setting is that in which we are pulled from the audience to take over from a juggler and find ourselves in the spotlight, paralyzed with fear. A variation would have the dreamer tossing the balls, hoops or skittles only to fumble and drop them to the jeers of the crowd. Such scenarios are typical for people who fear they have taken on too many commitments. To dream of being in the ring, or a cage, with wild animals, or of putting one's head in a lion's mouth reflects a fear of putting oneself in unnecessary danger, not an uncommon dream for someone who feels pressured into accepting a job for which he feels unqualified, or is in a relationship which he unconsciously suspects will savage him emotionally.

To watch wild animals performing tricks symbolizes the guilt of having stripped others of their dignity, perhaps by putting them down in front of colleagues or friends. If we see ourselves performing tricks at the whim of a sadistic ringmaster the dream may be reflecting a belief that we are being forced to live according to the dictates and expectations of others. To watch the clowns with a feeling of sadness indicates that we feel life is a sham and that other people are not to be trusted to show their true feelings. Enjoyment of the rides at a carnival or funfair suggests the repression of a sensualist nature. A terrifying ride would indicate a fear of losing control of events.

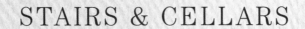

STAIRS & CELLARS

Stairs link levels of consciousness and are generally symbolic of progress or the desire to make progress. The question you need to consider is whether the stairs in your dream were narrow or wide, winding or straight, steep, grand and imposing or merely austere and functional. In the dreamscape the ideal stairs are wide and easy to climb or descend. If you find yourself stuck halfway with no sense of whether to go up or down, this suggests indecision, fear of commitment and lack of progress. Descending a flight of stairs to the ground floor should not be seen as negative, but simply as a return to a normal state of awareness.

Being a part of the structure of a building, stairs are frequently representative of a dreamer's attitude to home life. Narrow stairs imply restriction, while grand staircases symbolize flamboyance and freedom to express emotions at home. A staircase with bare boards indicates either that something within the family unit is unresolved or something in the house itself remains unfinished. A functionally carpeted staircase might imply a current situation or relationship which is regarded by the dreamer as either temporary or lacking any emotional depth. A plush, luxuriously carpeted staircase suggests the dreamer has a feeling of security and contentment at home.

Rooms below ground level symbolize repressed impulses, primitive instincts and our deepest fears. That is one reason why we all share a fear of what might lie hidden in the shadows of a cellar. Basements also have a physical association with the stomach and bowels. So, if there is a boiler which has broken down or is straining to capacity, it could be that the dream is warning against over-indulging in food to compensate for a lack of affection or interest in life.

TREES

Trees are universal symbols reflecting the phases of human life: the embryo is represented by the seed, youth envisaged in terms of 'blossoming' and 'branching out' and maturity symbolized in the production of fruit or new seed (that is a family of our own). Many cultures, philosophies and religious traditions have adopted the tree as a symbol of the belief that human beings are the connecting point of celestial and terrestrial forces: man is envisaged as the trunk of the tree with branches stretching to the heavens and roots penetrating the ground.

A single tree featuring prominently in a dream is therefore likely to symbolize the individual, his or her family (as reflected in the expression 'a family tree') or the human 'family' and its various 'branches'. A single oak, or any tree associated with strength or having a phallic shape, will represent a specific male. A fragrant flowering fruit or ornamental tree can be symbolic of a specific female. If the tree is ancient and awe-inspiring it could be a sign of the symbolic awakening of the dreamer's Higher Self and sense of union with the universal creative force.

On another level, wandering among trees in a forest can represent a curiosity about the nature of the unconscious. Wood is another symbol of the unconscious, it being derived from a living, growing source which remains impenetrable to the conscious mind.

GARDENS

Gardens can reveal a lot about temperament. A tidy, formal garden symbolizes someone organized but perhaps a little rigid and predictable. A sprawling cottage garden suggests an effusive but casual personality who leaves things to take their own course, perhaps due to earlier disappointments.

A vegetable garden or orchard implies a down-to-earth personality. If either is merely a notable feature, it suggests the dreamer has one eye on the future and is prepared for sudden changes. A productive plot of home-grown fruit or vegetables can also symbolize the dreamer's desire to 'be fruitful' and raise children. In fact, what is being cultivated can be as significant as the act of cultivation. Citrus fruits, for example, might symbolize a sharp tongue or bitterness towards someone else. Herbs represent the wish for a healthier lifestyle. Common vegetables such as carrots, leeks or potatoes symbolize the urge to establish roots and provide the basic necessities of a stable family life.

A profusion of weeds symbolizes problems which are being neglected and allowed to take root in the unconscious. Dreaming of uprooting weeds or cultivating an overgrown patch is symbolic of the dreamer's desire to make a fresh start in life, to take control of destructive habits and for more creative and productive means of self-expression. If the same ground is being dug over and over again, this suggests a preoccupation with a problem which we can not accept has been resolved or is now beyond our control. If the problem involves a barrier to your ambitions or a residue of feelings which you want to be rid of, imagine it in the form of a thorn bush, large weed or nettle, which you dig up and burn, leaving the ashes to blow away.

SUN

The sun is the primary symbol of the active masculine principle and of the source of life. As such it has been an image for heightened awareness, wisdom and spiritual illumination since ancient times. For a woman to dream of the sun is often symbolic of her awakening animus or masculine qualities, although the image can also refer to her father, a brother, son or male partner. For a man the sun can symbolize his father, a brother or close male friend, but is more likely to reflect a growing understanding of the world and the fulfilment of his paternal instincts. To dream of the rising sun is a sign that a new phase of your life is beginning or of the birth of new ideas. Such a dream can also be a reminder to someone who is depressed that no matter how bleak the present situation might appear, the source of life is ever present and that a 'new day will dawn' with new opportunities.

To see the setting sun is to accept that a phase of your life is over. To dream of the sun reflecting in water suggests that you have achieved a balance between the forces of action and emotion in yourself, or that at an unconscious level you have accepted a female partner (symbolized by the water) as reflecting your light without extinguishing your energy. To see the sun partly obscured by clouds is symbolic of temporary difficulties, but hints at the dreamer's ability to look beyond them and imagine a successful outcome. But the sun also has its negative aspect. Dreaming of a sunscorched garden is likely to be reminding the man who prides himself on being practical and physical that all growing things need water (that is, nurturing the emotions) and a spell in the shade (that is, rest) if they are to thrive and grow straight (that is, balanced). Be aware, too, that in dreams the sun can illuminate the darkest corners of the unconscious, although it will only do this in order to help us fully understand ourselves.

FIRE

Dreams featuring fire are usually of a destructive and disturbing nature with the dreamer fleeing as his or her house burns to the ground. Fire can also be seen as a purifying force. If fire reduces your dream-house to ashes, interpret it as an exorcism of some out-moded ideas and attitudes or as a rather heavy-handed hint that it is time to move on! In the dreamscape fire is also a symbol of the light of knowledge and awareness illuminating the darkness of ignorance. If you find yourself searching through a strangely familiar house in the dark with only a torch to light your way, it is likely that you are looking to discover previously hidden aspects of your personality.

Alternatively, you might finally be looking to shed light on long-neglected memories as symbolized by the cobwebbed recesses of the rooms. Take careful consideration of the symbolic significance of the decor and style of the room, or the objects which you find may reveal the true meaning of the dream. As a symbol of the hearth at the heart of the house, a dream of fire can be recalling the emotional warmth and security of the family home. Such a dream may also symbolize the flaring up of passions to comfort, scar or consume both lover and beloved. The size and intensity of the fire should give further clues as to which of these situations is apt. A bonfire can be a very revealing image if you can recall who lit it and who is represented by the dummy, or 'Guy', which is invariably to be found on top of the pile!

Fire and water are traditionally thought to be mutually exclusive, with water extinguishing fire and fire transforming water to steam, symbolizing conflict or dying passion. However, in the dreamscape, if flames are reflected in water the dream is drawing the attention to the idea that the active male aspect of the dreamer and his or her passive feminine aspect are balanced and should be considered as complementary.

THE SEASONS

Spring is the universal symbol of rebirth, vitality and hope. If a dream with a spring setting occurs while you are going through a troubled time, it may be reminding you of the momentum for change and growth within each of us which will overcome even the most discouraging conditions. Dreams of spring or those with prominent symbols of the season are prompts from the unconscious to start new ventures.

Long, hot summer days are synonymous with relaxation, cloudless blue skies, gardens bursting with vibrant colour and the intense heat of the sun. Dreams with a summer setting are symbolic of satisfaction, achievement, revitalizing energies and clear horizons. If the dream does not follow a specific success, such as passing an exam or a promotion, then it may reflect an inner sense of infinite possibilities ahead.

Autumn is traditionally the season of harvesting and of reaping what one has sown. Dreams of autumn are usually rich with vivid fiery colours, particularly orange, which corresponds to the sacral chakra in Eastern philosophy, an energy centre in the groin, which emphasizes the theme of procreation. Images of falling leaves suggest that it might be prudent to conserve our energy and resources in preparation for the possibility of dark, stormy times ahead.

In general, winter scenes symbolize a withdrawal into the self, as reflected in the animal's instinct to hibernate and man's urge to stay indoors. The cold weather and dark days can symbolize either sexual or psychological frigidity. In the latter case the unconscious could be warning that a vital part of the personality is in danger of being 'frozen out' because it is being denied by the ego. Perhaps it might suggest something in danger of becoming an obsession should be 'frozen' for the time being because it cannot be fully understood in our present state of mind. In this case winter imagery is being used to emphasize the importance of rest and reflection above action.